Love, Joy, Peace, Patience, Kindness, Goodness, Faithfulness, Gentleness, Self-control. Love, Joy, Peace, Patience, Kindness, Goodness, Faithfulness, Gentleness, Self-control. Love, Joy, Peace, Patience, Kindness, Goodness, Faithfulness, Gentleness, Self-control. Love, Joy, Peace, Patience, Kindness, Goodness, Faithfulness, Gentleness, Self-control. Love, Joy, Peace, Patience, Kindness, Goodness, Faithfulness, Gentleness, Self-control. Love, Joy, Peace, Patience, Kindness, Goodness, Faithfulness, Gentleness, Self-control. Love, Joy, Peace, Patience, Kindness, Goodness, Faithfulness, Gentleness, Self-control. Love, Joy, Peace, Patience, Kindness, Goodness, Faithfulness, Gentleness, Self-control.

This journal of devotional experiences belongs to:

_____

Love. Joy. Peace. Patience. Kindness. Goodness. Faithfulness. Gentleness. Self-control.

Tasting the Fruit of the Spirit: 30 Devotional Experiences

Visit our Web site: **www.grouppublishing.com**

Credits
Contributing Writers: Jenny Baker, Debbie Gowensmith, Mikal Keefer,
Joy-Elizabeth Lawrence, and Cheryl Penner
Editor: Kelli B. Trujillo
Creative Development Editor: Amy Simpson
Chief Creative Officer: Joani Schultz
Copy Editor: Loma Huh
Cover Art Director: Jeff Storm
Cover Designer: Liz Howe Design
Cover Photography: Daniel Treat
Art Director: Jean Bruns
Interior Design: Toolbox Creative
Production Manager: Dodie Tipton

ISBN 0-7644-2515-3

10 9 8 7 6 5 4 3 2 1   12 11 10 09 08 07 06 05 04 03
Printed in Singapore.

Love. Joy. Peace. Patience. Kindness. Goodness. Faithfulness. Gentleness. Self-control.

This is more than just a recipe for having good manners. It's more than just a prescription for happiness. These characteristics are 100 percent counter-cultural—completely opposite of how the world around you lives.

They're the natural fruit that springs forth and grows in your life as a result of the Holy Spirit's presence within you. They're your Christian ID card. They're your spiritual DNA.

If you're a Christian, then you've probably already gotten a taste of this Spirit fruit…but not like this. In *Tasting the Fruit of the Spirit,* you'll explore these characteristics at a whole new level. In each of these thirty devotions, you'll have a chance to *do* something that will help you get a new perspective on God's spiritual fruit in your life. You'll study a Scripture passage that challenges you and gives you greater insight. You'll have space to journal your own ideas, questions, and experiences. You'll be changed.

And as you come to understand the fruit of the Spirit more deeply, you'll notice that same fruit growing more evidently in your life. By watching how you live and grow, by seeing your Christlikeness, *others* will want to "taste and see that the Lord is good" (Psalm 34:8).

Tasting the Fruit of the Spirit

The Whole Letter

Find a letter—one you've never read before. Now, let your eyes fall on two sentences. Read them. Think about what you read. Does it make sense? Do you understand the situation, the relationship between the writer and recipient? Imagine all the scenarios that could result from the two sentences you read.

Now, read the entire letter. Do you better understand those two sentences? Do you recognize a relationship, a problem, an emotion?

Now, read Galatians 5:22-23. Think about these verses. Why did Paul write this? Do you think that you will understand these verses better by reading the whole letter of Galatians? Take the time to do so, perhaps even out loud. (Letters such as Galatians were commonly read aloud because they were a message for the whole church.)

As you read, notice the contrast of "the acts of the sinful nature" (Galatians 5:19) to the fruit of the Spirit. Why are they called fruit? Why is Paul discussing this?

The Galatians were being taught by false teachers that salvation came through following the old laws. Paul disagreed, saying, "Did you receive the Spirit by observing the law, or by believing what you heard?" (Galatians 3:2). He lists the fruit of the Spirit because *those* are the evidence of following the Spirit of God, not going through the motions of rule keeping.

Healthy trees bear fruit naturally. Think of the Spirit fruit.

Love. Joy. Peace. Patience. Kindness. Goodness. Faithfulness. Gentleness. Self-control.

Do you bear these naturally? Prepare your heart to learn more about what this fruit can mean in your life.

What I saw, noticed, questioned, felt, read, thought, experienced:

[Galatians 5:22-23]

ns 5:22-

[write something]

write

Love. Joy. Peace. Patience. Kindness. Goodness. Faithfulness. Gentleness. Self-control.

Following Rules

Read Galatians 4:8-11. What kind of "weak and miserable principles" were the Galatians turning back to?

Read Deuteronomy 22:10-12 for a sample. The first few books of the Old Testament are full of rules God gave his people—in order to establish a covenant between God and Israel. But people broke God's rules; none could become holy. Read Galatians 3:21-25.

Imagine trying to follow those laws you read about in Deuteronomy 22. Look at the tags on the clothing in your closet. What would you have left to wear if you could only wear clothing made of a single fiber? Think about how different your life would be if your salvation depended upon following the rules.

Could you follow this rule? Could you follow other rules in the Old Testament? Would you be afraid of messing up? Would you be stressed out trying to remember everything? Would you follow the rules because you loved God or because you were expected to obey?

Since Jesus came into the world and sent the Holy Spirit, the outside evidence of faith has changed. Rather than being people who follow rules, we are people who follow the Spirit. The fruit of the Spirit is evidence of a life in the Spirit.

Read Galatians 5:22-23 again. Pray that this fruit will be evident in your life. Thank God for the gift of Jesus and the presence of the Spirit. Thank God for what Paul says in Galatians 5:18: "If you are led by the Spirit, you are not under law."

What I saw, noticed, questioned, felt, read, thought, experienced:

[write something]

le principles

Love. Joy. Peace. Patience. Kindness. Goodness. Faithfulness. Gentleness. Self-control.

God's Sacrificial Love

"You are what you eat." Yikes! Have you ever read the ingredients of the food you put inside your body?

Get your hands on your very favorite snack food—a candy bar, potato chips, a doughnut, or those "fruit" snacks created to convince us that raspberries are blue. Now for the moment of truth…read the list of ingredients. What do you find? Are the ingredients healthy? Are they pure and wholesome? (If they are, you must have been out of double chocolate snack cakes.)

Still, despite what you found, you like the snack, don't you? Even though you know what's inside, your mouth is watering for just a taste, right? Go ahead, indulge. Despite what we find on the inside of some foods, we still love them.

That same concept—loving something despite some inner ugliness—applies to God's relationship with you. Despite your best efforts, you are not always the nicest, purest, most wholesome person you can be. None of us are.

Read 1 John 4:7-10. How do these verses define *love?* How do you know that God loves you? What does the fact that God's only Son died for you say about God's understanding of your sin?

Think about your own "list of ingredients"—times you've shown love and times you've shown ugliness. Now read 1 John 4:9-10 again.

God knows you, understands you, and is fully aware that you have some ugly stuff inside. But God loves you anyway. So much that Jesus died for you.

What I saw, noticed, questioned, felt, read, thought, experienced:

Love. Joy. Peace. Patience. Kindness. Goodness. Faithfulness. Gentleness. Self-control.

efine LOVE

Valuing God

"I love that CD!"

"I love that shirt!"

"I love that car!"

We often express our "love" for material things because they're valuable to us. What do you value?

Now think a little harder about it. Ask yourself this classic question: If your house were destroyed by a fire or natural disaster and you could only take three things with you, what would you take? What's most valuable to you? Jewelry, a car, the stuffed horse your dad gave to you when you were two?

Now go get at least one of those items. Touch it, smell it, look carefully at it. Can you assign it a dollar value? Or is it priceless? Would others assign it a similar value? Why or why not?

What the world values may be drastically different from what you value. For example, consider the Apostle Paul's early life. He had an education. He had social standing. He had technical correctness. But he didn't have Christ.

Read Philippians 3:7-11. When he learned about Christ's sacrificial love, Paul gave up everything of worldly value to love Christ. For the rest of his life, Paul served Jesus out of love for him.

Realizing just how much God loves us may drive us to our knees, as Paul could attest. In response to God's love, what wells up in us is a love for God that is humble, grateful, loyal, and radical. The world turns upside down. We no longer value the things we used to value.

Think through your mental list again. Meditate on your love for God. Where does God fit in that list? Paul found that his love for Christ became the most valuable thing in his world—more valuable, even, than his own life.

What I saw, noticed, questioned, felt, read, thought, experienced:

[write]

Love. Joy. Peace. Patience. Kindness. Goodness. Faithfulness. Gentleness. Self-control.

Philippians 3:7-11

Neighborly Love

The parable of the good Samaritan—perhaps you've heard it before. No matter. Read it again in Luke 10:25-37. This time, think about how the Samaritan was able to be so good.

Perhaps a little background info would help. The Samaritan broke social rules by interacting with the beaten man. He also took a physical risk; the robbers still could have been hiding. He took on the financial burden of caring for the man, too. What kind of person does all that for someone he doesn't even know?

The kind of person who loves others with the love of God.

God loves each of us unconditionally. He created each of us with inestimable intrinsic value and worth. Can you learn to see others, and so to love them, the way God sees and loves them?

As an experiment, choose someone, anyone, to follow around for an hour. Devote that hour to serving the person. Pick up after your sloppy kid brother. Make phone calls and pay the bills for your mom. Help your grandpa organize his tackle box.

After the hour, read Luke 10:25-37 again. Reflect upon what it means to love others as God loves them—to love them so much that you serve them, look out for their interest, respond to their needs, and even sacrifice for them. What kind of a person does that?

With the love of God, *you* do.

What I saw, noticed, questioned, felt, read, thought, experienced:

Luke 10:25-37

[write]

Love. Joy. Peace. Patience. Kindness. Goodness. Faithfulness. Gentleness. Self-control.

Resonance

Put a little water into a crystal glass or goblet. Now wet your finger and run it around the top of the glass until it "sings." You can see the water vibrating when you do this. The glass sings because the action of your finger makes it vibrate at its natural frequency—which is called resonance. Don't worry if you don't understand it! Think of it as your finger creating the same song as the secret song hidden in the heart of the glass—and because you've hit the right note, the song becomes audible.

Read and enjoy Psalm 92.

Joy is like the note hidden in the glass. Joy is tuning in to what God is doing around you, seeing the world through his eyes, picking up on his delight in us as his children. Anyone can find happiness for a while—through laughing at a joke or buying something new. Happiness depends on what is happening to you. Joy is different; joy goes deeper. Joy is when your whole being sings because you have caught a glimpse of God at work. Joy can creep up on you and surprise you in unexpected places.

So breathe deeply, tune in. Listen for the song that God is singing and let it echo in your heart. Sing for joy at the work of his hands.

What I saw, noticed, questioned, felt, read, thought, experienced:

Love. **Joy.** Peace. Patience. Kindness. Goodness. Faithfulness. Gentleness. Self-control.

Watch some advertisements on TV. They probably include lots of happy people, smiling and enjoying life. If you can't get to a TV, flip through a glossy magazine and look at the ads there. What are the things that these ads tell you will make you happy? Nice clothes, a slim figure, a new car, the right breakfast cereal? Do you believe them? Are they right?

Read 1 Peter 1:3-9.

Peter obviously never watched these advertisements. He had a completely different perspective of where joy comes from.

In the middle of difficult times, as an unlikely companion to grief, joy can penetrate even our darkest moments. Joy begins in your heart and seeps to every part of your being, until you are so full that joy leaks out. Joy helps you to see the point of difficult times because it reminds you of Jesus and of your future inheritance.

Are you going through a difficult time? Are you tempted to buy into the advertisements offer of fleeting happiness? Read these verses again—what has Jesus already done for you? What do you have to look forward to? Start to thank Jesus for what he has done, and be prepared to be surprised by joy.

HAPPINESS IS A

What I saw, noticed, questioned, felt, read, thought, experienced:

e happy and write!

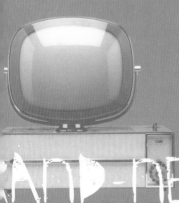

AND-NEW CAR!!??

Love. **Joy.** Peace. Patience. Kindness. Goodness. Faithfulness. Gentleness. Self-control.

Report Cards

Dig out an old school report card and look at the grades. (If your report cards were never that good or if you can't locate one, find an award that you have won or a certificate for something that you have achieved.) Remember what you had to do to get that grade or award. How did you feel when you first got your report card? Was all the work worth it? What did your parents say? How long did the feeling last?

Read Acts 16:25-34.

When the earthquake hit that prison, the jailer thought his life was no longer worth living. He was responsible for all the prisoners and expected them to take the opportunity to escape. He thought he had failed; he was ready to die.

And yet, his despair was turned into utter joy—read verse 34 again. Instead of the end of his career, he found the beginning of true life. His joy came not from the fact that all the prisoners were still there, but from the fact that two of those prisoners introduced him to Jesus.

It's great to get good grades. It's satisfying when you achieve things and get rewarded for it. But true joy comes not from your effort or what you achieve. True joy comes from that life-changing experience of meeting Jesus. Take some time to thank Jesus that you have met him. Thank him for what he has done in your life. And feel the joy warm your heart and put a smile on your face.

Read Acts 16:25-34.

_____ *What I saw, noticed, questioned, felt, read, thought, experienced:*

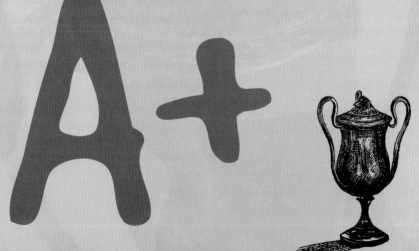

WRITE SOMETHING BRILLIANT

A+

Love. **Joy.** Peace. Patience. Kindness. Goodness. Faithfulness. Gentleness. Self-control.

Peace in Suffering

Sit cross-legged on the floor, or kneel—whichever is less comfortable. The goal is for you to be distracted by pain, but not so much that you can't focus. Ready? Good—now keep reading.

In your life there's happiness and there's peace. They're not the same.

Happiness (and relief!) is what you'll feel when you stretch your legs and feel the blood begin circulating again. Happiness is all about circumstances.

But peace is something deeper.

Just ask Stephen.

If anyone had a right to be distracted by his circumstances, and anxious about his immediate future, it was Stephen.

He'd just finished explaining to the very people who had demanded Jesus be killed that they'd made a tremendous error. They dragged Stephen outside the city walls and were gathering rocks so they could stone him to death.

In short, things weren't looking good.

But through it all, even facing his attackers, Stephen displayed not anger or fear, but rather...peace.

Read Acts 6:8–7:59. See how Stephen kept his eyes on Jesus. How he focused on pleasing his audience of One more than the audience of man that moved in on him like a pack of wolves.

Do you, like Stephen, experience peace during times of discomfort? during poverty, illness, or tragedy?

Now get comfortable. (Ahh! Can you feel your feet again?)

Stephen kept his eyes on Jesus—and found peace.

Where are you looking?

Acts 6:8–7:

What I saw, noticed, questioned, felt, read, thought, experienced:

Love. Joy. **Peace.** Patience. Kindness. Goodness. Faithfulness. Gentleness. Self-control.

PEACE

[write]

HAPPINESS

Peace Announcement

The phone isn't always an instrument of peace.

Yes, it's one way your friends stay in touch. And it's a great way to get good news—the next call *could* be the one announcing you're the Grand Prize winner in the Gazillion Dollar Giveaway.

But the phone also can deliver challenges.

The next call might tell you a close friend is moving across the country. That a grandparent has cancer. That an accident has changed your life forever.

There's no shortage of pain in the world, and sooner or later your share will find you—maybe by phone.

When that call comes, how will you respond?

Some people hang up, then shuffle through their days as the walking wounded. Others flare into anger. Some self-medicate to numb the pain with drugs, drink, food, or sex.

And some experience and move through their pain with a peaceful, clear purpose that astounds their friends.

Read Jesus' words in John 14:27-31.

Jesus gives us peace that survives tough times, that frees us from anxiety and fear.

Now take a moment and change the message on your answering machine. For the next 24 hours, instead of a simple "leave a message at the beep," let callers experience a message of peace.

Add a line or two to your message that prompts callers to think about authentic peace and where it comes from. Quote part of what Jesus said, or ask callers to pray for peace in their lives.

If nothing else, you'll give a few telemarketers a memorable call.

What I saw, noticed, questioned, felt, read, thought, experienced:

[write HERE]

Peace on Earth

Fill a clear bottle halfway with water, then add an inch or so of cooking oil. Screw the lid on tightly.

Now shake the bottle to mix the oil and water. Set the bottle down and watch what happens. No matter how well you sloshed and shook the ingredients together, the oil will work its way up through the water to form a separate layer. Wait long enough and it will look as if you never mixed the oil and water at all.

Oil and water naturally repel each other. They're simply incompatible.

There are nations in the world that seem to have Oil and Water Syndrome. They can't seem to find common ground. They refuse to be at peace. They've learned to live with perpetual conflict.

Even when negotiations prompt a cease-fire, there isn't lasting peace.

Peace—*true* peace—isn't just a lack of conflict. It's the presence of God.

Read Luke 2:8-15 aloud. Whisper the words: "...on earth peace to men on whom his favor rests."

Those words were an announcement that God had invaded history. God wasn't just recommending peace—he had come to show what it looked like. He had sent his Son.

Now say the words again, loudly. Proclaim them like you're announcing them to the world: "On earth peace to men on whom his favor rests."

Listen to your words ring out.

Can there be peace on earth between nations? The headlines would say the answer is no, and maybe the headlines are right.

But there *can* be peace in your life.

What I saw, noticed, questioned, felt, read, thought, experienced:

[write something]

Love. Joy. **Peace.** Patience. Kindness. Goodness. Faithfulness. Gentleness. Self-control.

Find a saltshaker or packet of salt. Spill enough on a tabletop to create a dime-sized drift.

Sweeping it onto the floor would take you about three seconds. But that's not what you're going to do. You're going to put it back in the shaker (or packet)—one grain at a time.

Now do you wish you didn't bite your nails?

Something so simple…but so time consuming. Accomplishing the task takes concentration. And patience.

We're not, by nature, a patient species. We want our needs and desires met—*now*. Things that take patience, we delegate to others or avoid altogether.

But God is willing to put in the time to do things right—including building us into the people he knows we can be. When we partner with God, we've got to move at his timing, and that forces us to be patient.

Read 2 Peter 3:7-9.

We share the gospel with a friend and want to see a response—now.

We start a new diet and then stare into the mirror to see results—now.

We punch up a favorite Web site and expect to be connected—now.

But "now" is highly overrated. It's convenient but narrow. Some things can and will happen in and through you only if you move at God's pace.

Patience. Your job isn't to run ahead of God, blazing a trail someplace he doesn't necessarily want to send you. Your job is to faithfully follow.

Be patient.

Be patient.

[write something]

Love. Joy. Peace. **Patience.** Kindness. Goodness. Faithfulness. Gentleness. Self-control.

When we partner with God, we've got to move at his timing.

The Waiting Game

Take a look at your watch or situate yourself near a clock. What time is it? What time will it be in ten minutes? Mentally fix your mind on that time ten minutes from now. Now wait for it to come. As you wait, keep reading.

All Hannah wanted was a baby.

She was willing. Her husband, Elkanah, was willing.

And when you consider that God called an entire universe into being, you wouldn't think it a major strain for God to nudge Hannah's barren womb and let her get pregnant.

But Hannah waited. And waited. And waited.

Year after empty year she felt the ache of her loss. And year after year, living in a culture where a large part of her worth was her ability to give Elkanah a son, she endured the ridicule of those around her.

Yet she continued to pray, continued to ask for a child.

Then, the impossible happened: God gave her a son.

And Hannah gave the son, Samuel, back to God.

Read 1 Samuel 1:1-20.

Hannah's story is one of faithful patience, of waiting for God's timing. God knew the precise moment Hannah would first hold a son in her grateful arms. But it's not information God shared with Hannah.

What God required of Hannah was precise what he requires of you: patience.

Patience as God's plan for your life unfolds

Patience as God acts in your life to mature you.

Patience as God works through you to accomplish his will in your world.

As you wait for the clock to arrive at the tim you set your mind on, reflect on how this is like waiting on God's timing in your life.

Be patient. Faithfully patient.

[write something]

Love. Joy. Peace. **Patience.** Kindness. Goodness. Faithfulness. Gentleness. Self-control.

What time is it? What time will it be in ten minutes?

Get comfortable—this could take awhile.

Count the hairs on your head. Not all of them, just fifty. If you can't see them, use a mirror.

Still too tough? Then recruit a friend (not one who's bald—that's cheating) and see how long it takes you to accurately count 50 hairs…150 hairs…200 hairs.

You could be here all *day,* right?

Now think of how patient you'd have to be to count the hairs on the heads of everyone in your family…in your school…in your town.

That's patience.

And it's the sort of patience God has. Read Luke 12:6-8.

God's patience isn't just a tolerance for doing mundane tasks. Read the passage again, carefully. You'll see that God's patience is motivated by love.

The patience the Holy Spirit wants to build in you is *loving* patience. It's more than the ability to bite your tongue and stay civil when yet again your sister takes forever in the bathroom and makes you late for school.

It's *loving* your sister—even though she makes you late.

It's *loving* your classmate—even though he doesn't finish his half of the report in time.

It's *loving* your boss—though you didn't get the hours you wanted.

Anyone can wait. It's easy. Even dead people can do it.

But not everyone can love patiently.

That's patience.

What I saw, noticed, questioned, felt, read, thought, experienced:

[write something]

Love. Joy. Peace. **Patience.** Kindness. Goodness. Faithfulness. Gentleness. Self-control.

ntdown

Just Like You

Sit in a busy place—maybe a train station or a shopping mall—anywhere with lots of people coming and going.

Watch the people walking past. Can you tell anything about them? Who looks happy, worried, in need? Who would you like to get to know better?

Now think about what you have in common with the people you see. You breathe air, eat food, need God, have friends—what else? Think about all the experiences you share with these people you have never even spoken to. How does that make you feel?

Read Luke 7:36-50.

This is a beautiful, tender moment in the life of Jesus. Just before he faces betrayal and crucifixion, he receives the extravagant worship of a woman who knows she is forgiven. And what does Simon think? Read verse 39 again.

He sneers at her and labels her a sinner. "If Jesus only knew what kind of person she is…

But Jesus did know—she was the kind of person who needed love and forgiveness—just like Simon, just like everyone else.

Kindness is recognizing the humanity of others—that we are just like them. Kindness goes beyond outward appearances and labels, and sees that underneath we are all created by God and in need of his love. Kindness accepts people, regardless of what they have done.

So look again at the people around you. Look with kindness, and see yourself reflected in their faces.

Just Like You

[write someth

Love. Joy. Peace. Patience. **Kindness.** Goodness. Faithfulness. Gentleness. Self-control.

Gardening

Go outside and take care of your yard—pull up some weeds, prune some plants, mow the lawn, sweep up leaves. You may want to ask for some advice if you have never done it before! If you *don't* have a garden or yard, then water your houseplants, go and help a neighbor, or see if you can pull some weeds growing in sidewalk cracks.

When you take care of plants, they grow. If you create the right conditions for them, they flourish, sending out new shoots, bearing fruit and flowers. Pulling weeds create a safe environment for healthy plants to grow.

Read Ruth 2:1-23.

Boaz showed great kindness to Ruth by creating safe conditions in which she could work. Read the passage again, and notice how he did this. He could have just taken over and given her grain to take home—but he didn't. He allowed her dignity in her work, the chance to provide for herself and Naomi. And like the plants under your care, Ruth flourished under his kindness.

Think of people you know who are working hard but may be struggling a little. How can you demonstrate kindness by showing them encouragement? Can you change the environment they work in and help them achieve their dreams? Ask God to show you what part you can play, and be prepared to help them grow with your kindness.

What I saw, noticed, questioned, felt, read, thought, experienced:

[write something]

On the Lookout

Go on a short walk outside. As you're walking, be on the lookout...for forgotten coins on the ground, for dropped or overlooked papers, for discarded cans or candy wrappers.

Do you normally pay attention to those things? If you weren't looking for them, would you notice them? Would you have seen that penny near the edge of the sidewalk? Would the bubble gum wrapper have caught your eye?

Probably not. It takes an intentional vigilance—a purposeful watchfulness.

God's kindness is like that.

Read 2 Samuel 9:1-13.

Now read verse 1 again. David was on the lookout. He found a way to demonstrate God's kindness.

David found out about Mephibosheth, the grandson of a man who spent years trying to kill him, and showed him extravagant kindness.

Now reread verse 8. Mephibosheth was shocked that David even *noticed* him. He called himself a "dead dog." He'd been crippled all his life. He'd probably felt discarded, overlooked and forgotten by society...like a coin on the side of the road. Yet David changed everything. He invited Mephibosheth into his household and treated him like his very own son.

God's Spirit enables you to exhibit that same sort of kindness. Kindness that moves beyond reacting to a need to actually *seeking out* needs.

Through God's Spirit, you, too, can live out kindness that's on the lookout—always observant, aware, open-eyed, open-eared—for overlooked people or unnoticed needs.

What I saw, noticed, questioned, felt, read, thought, experienced:

[write something]

Love. Joy. Peace. Patience. **Kindness.** Goodness. Faithfulness. Gentleness. Self-control.

Without Limits

Go fly a kite. Feel the pulling of the kite on the string. Think about the limits the kite will have for as long as you hold it. That string keeps it bound to a certain area, a specific radius. It isn't free to soar any direction, any distance.

Yet God's goodness has no limits. There's no string holding it back. His goodness is boundless, and it shows in everything he does.

Read Psalm 103:1-22.

In this psalm, David has experienced God's goodness and expresses how far-reaching it is. He speaks of God as forgiving, compassionate, satisfying, never changing, loving forever.

God is the definition of goodness—it is his very being. We never need to doubt the goodness of his plan for us—it can *only* be good. His goodness doesn't change—it is inalterable.

How good do you think you are as a person? Do you ever feel frustrated, as if something is holding you back from producing goodness in your life?

Because of God's unending love and forgiveness, when we allow God's Spirit to move in our lives, the Spirit draws from his own unlimited resources to produce goodness in our lives…goodness without limits.

go fly a kite.

What I saw, noticed, questioned, felt, read, thought, experienced:

[write something]

Love. Joy. Peace. Patience. Kindness. **Goodness.** Faithfulness. Gentleness. Self-control.

Use a thermometer to determine your body's temperature. If you've ever been to the doctor's office or the hospital, you know how important your temperature is. Average body temperature is 98.6 degrees Fahrenheit; any significant fluctuation higher or lower can speak volumes, warning of the possibility of a multitude of potential problems, such as stress, infection, or hormone imbalance.

Read Genesis 6:5-22.

What did Noah use as a standard to evaluate the goodness of his actions? In his day, the world was so corrupt that he was the *only* good, upright, and blameless man. Sinful lifestyles were the norm, but did Noah adjust his standards to match those of the culture around him?

Noah didn't cave under the pressure of other people. No matter how much goodness his life demonstrated in comparison with those around him, he let God's Spirit be his "goodness thermometer."

How is the goodness temperature in your life? Are there things you need to change to line up with God's standard? When you let God's Spirit guide you, you can learn to evaluate your choices and actions, and pure and good results will be produced.

Do you think Noah felt alone in his convictions and grew tired of standing for God in the face of ridicule? Do you ever feel alone in your decisions that demonstrate goodness?

Read Galatians 6:9.

Remember the blessings God has promised as you continue in goodness, according to God's standards.

A Fragrant Offering

Find the worst-smelling thing you can think of, and smell it for as long as you can stand it. (Try onions, the garbage can, or even those sweaty socks on your floor.) Stop before you get lightheaded.

Next find the best-smelling thing you can think of, and take a few good whiffs of it. (This might be perfume, chocolate, or flowers.)

Our sense of smell is very powerful. With it we're attracted to or repulsed by many things. A scent tells us much about an item and either draws us to it or turns us away from it.

Your life has an aroma. Will it be sweet-smelling or foul? attractive or repulsive?

God's Spirit can produce goodness in your life as a beautiful scent to those around you and to God.

Read Ephesians 4:25–5:7.

Are your actions demonstrating goodness in your everyday opportunities? Are you living peacefully with others, building up others in truth; or is your speech filled with bitterness, rage, slander, malice? Are you making the most of opportunities to be kind, compassionate, and to live a life of love? Do you flee from sexual immorality, impurity, greed, obscenity, foolish talk?

Read Ephesians 5:2 again.

Christ, our ultimate example, demonstrated goodness by sacrificing himself to be presented as a fragrant offering to God. What kind of scent is your life producing? When God's Spirit produces goodness in your life, demonstrated through your everyday choices, you will emanate a fragrant spiritual scent that is not only acceptable, but attracts others to you and to God.

A FRAGRANT OFFERIN

What I saw, noticed, questioned, felt, read, thought, experienced:

[write something]

A Fragrant Offering

Love. Joy. Peace. Patience. Kindness. **Goodness.** Faithfulness. Gentleness. Self-control.

Loyalty

Find some magnets—maybe you have some on your refrigerator, or perhaps you have a magnetic paper clip holder. Did you ever play with magnets when you were a child? Play with the magnets now. See if they magnetize other pieces of metal like paper clips or pins. Stick the magnets to the refrigerator and notice how some of them stick powerfully to the door. Others may be weaker. Open and close the refrigerator door. Do any magnets fall off? Are some magnets attracted or repelled by other magnets?

Read Proverbs 3:3. Is the magnetic attraction something binding?

What is faithfulness? Is it the same as loyalty, trustworthiness, constancy?

To whom or what should we be faithful? God? Family and friends? Things we're completely sure about? Things we're unsure about?

How can you be faithful? Imagine how faithfulness bound around your neck would feel. Would it be like a leash? Would it be heavy, a great responsibility? Or would it be more like a magnet on a refrigerator, naturally stuck there, not a burden?

Faithfulness implies commitment and loyalty. How are you faithful? How can you become more faithful?

It is easy to waver in one's faith. Some days may seem more full of faith than others, but faith cannot be acted upon by a whim. Think about the "loyalty" of the magnets. Are you that faithful?

Think about the "loyalty" of the magnets. Are you that faithful?

What I saw, noticed, questioned, felt, read, thought, experienced:

[write something]

Love. Joy. Peace. Patience. Kindness. Goodness. **Faithfulness.** Gentleness. Self-control.

What does it mean to be faithful to God? Read 2 Kings 18:1-8 and 20:1-11. During a succession of wicked kings, Hezekiah was a faithful follower of God. Reread 18:5-6 and 20:3.

These verses are important because of the way they contrast with the descriptions of other rulers in 1 Kings and 2 Kings. Many of the texts about them describe the evil they did in the eyes of the Lord. (Look up 2 Kings 21:2 for an example.) But Hezekiah did what was right. Second Kings 18:4 describes Hezekiah's obedience to God by removing the places of idolatry. Even the snake Moses had made during the Exodus was being used as an idol!

Later in his life Hezekiah was about to die. But through the reminder to God about his faithfulness, he received healing and an extended life. God's sign to Hezekiah was the miracle of moving back a shadow. Now think about this for a moment—the moving shadow meant the sunlight moved. That meant the planet actually moved! The day was extended by a measurable amount.

Most of us have lives quite different from Hezekiah. We are not kings, nor do we have opportunities to tear down places of idolatry. Prophets do not come to us and forewarn us of our deaths. We do not see a day miraculously extended.

But we can still remain faithful to God, just like Hezekiah. We can look to him as an example of a faithful servant of God. We can thank God for the sign he gave to Hezekiah and for the life he gives to us.

Find a watch or clock that has to be wound up in order to work. Move the clock back ten hours. Spend some time imagining that you are Hezekiah, given longer life by God. Imagine this miracle—the movement of earth, of the sun, of the entire solar system.

Pray that you, too, will remain faithful.

What does it mean to be faithful to God?

What I saw, noticed, questioned, felt, read, thought, experienced:

ITHFUL TO GOD?

[write something]

Love. Joy. Peace. Patience. Kindness. Goodness. **Faithfulness.** Gentleness. Self-control.

In the kitchen, find a powdered drink mix like lemonade or Kool-Aid (or some tea bags, if you prefer that). Make the drink, or boil water to make the tea. Once you've added the drink mix or tea bag, watch how the color swirls in the water. Something—sugar, color, flavor—is being added to the water. What would happen if you suddenly decided that you didn't want this drink; that you just wanted water? Would you be able to separate the tea or dissolved drink mix from the water? Not easily.

Read Ruth 1:1-18. Ruth was determined to be loyal to Naomi. The words she used are so powerful and binding that they are often used in wedding ceremonies today. Even though she would be traveling to another country where the people spoke a different language and worshipped a different God, Ruth was willing to follow her mother-in-law. She was persistent; she was faithful.

Would you be this loyal? Naomi had no one; her husband and sons were dead. Because of the society of the time, widows without sons were paupers. She had nothing, not even a young son to be the future husband of Ruth.

What would Ruth gain by following Naomi? Nothing that she knew of. She would probably never see her own family again.

Acquaintances come and go.

But Ruth was no acquaintance of Naomi. She was inseparable.

How do you view your relationships with others? Because our society is so different from Ruth's, you will probably never have opportunity like hers. But you can still be loyal to your friends and family. Though you may not leave them geographically, are you loyal to them by your everyday actions, or have you cut them off? You can live together and be unloyal; you can see others every day and not care.

Pray that you will remain faithful to your friends and family. Pray that during difficult relational times, this fruit will be evident in your heart and life.

What I saw, noticed, questioned, felt, read, thought, experienced:

[write something]

Love. Joy. Peace. Patience. Kindness. Goodness. **Faithfulness.** Gentleness. Self-control.

Power in Gentleness

Have you ever been to a riverbed or ocean? Have you seen the stones, worn smooth by th
constant movement of water? Slowly the daily movement, the watery friction, softens the
lines and crevices of rock.

Go to your closet and find your oldest, most well-worn pair of shoes. Look at the soles. Ar
they worn? Do they match anymore? Did they look like this when they were brand new? Thi
of all the places you've been in these shoes. Think of all the cement, asphalt, rocks, grass
and sand that they've trod upon. The wear crept up on them; it did not come in one day.

Read Proverbs 25:15. Compare the "gentle tongue" to the daily interaction of water and
rock, of ground and shoe.

Often, it is tempting to try to do something all at once. If you wanted to smooth a stone, y
could sand it or even blast away part of it. If you wanted your shoes to wear out (perhaps
to get a new pair?), you could pick at the sole or cut some of the stitches to speed up the
process of wear and tear.

Imagine trying to persuade a "ruler." (Perhaps a teacher, parent, or respected elder.) It's
easy to jump in and loudly proclaim our rights. It's easy to point out wrongs and demand
fairness. But that is not always the best idea. Sometimes it takes gentleness—daily wear,
a gentle tongue.

Are you gentle in your speech? Not only is gentleness Christlike, it's also wise. It works,
often more than harsh language or clever, angry comments.

Gentleness can be evident in many ways. Pray today that the Holy Spirit will make
gentleness evident through your speech, through your interaction with others.

Gentleness

What I saw, noticed, questioned, felt, read, thought, experienced:

[write something]

Love. Joy. Peace. Patience. Kindness. Goodness. Faithfulness. **Gentleness.** Self-control.

Gentle Rest

What makes you tired? What makes you want a rest?

Find two very large books. (You could use a large phone book, dictionary, encyclopedia, or photo album.) Stand, arms outstretched, palms up, with one book on each hand. Hold them as long as you can.

When you can't hold the books anymore, put your arms down. Are you tired? Do your arms ache?

Read Matthew 11:28-30. Verse 28 is very popular, but focus again on verse 29. Jesus says to learn from him. What should we learn? Should we learn from his gentleness and humbleness of heart?

Write down some of your burdens—temptations, difficult relationships, choices you have to make—and place them upon your two big books. Hold the books again—this time until it's too hard, until you possibly could not do it anymore. (Don't hurt yourself.) Now, imagine giving these burdens to Jesus, the gentle one, the one who gives rest to your soul.

How does Jesus respond to your burdens? As you learn from Jesus, how will you respond to others' burdens? Having burdens makes rest for the soul unlikely. Often people who do not know Jesus will share with others—even confess, though they may not call it that. This is one way people try to ease their burdens. Will you listen? Will you be gentle?

{ Gentle Rest }

What I saw, noticed, questioned, felt, read, thought, experienced:

[write something]

Love. Joy. Peace. Patience. Kindness. Goodness. Faithfulness. **Gentleness.** Self-control.

How does Jesus respond to your burdens?

Whisper

Have you ever wondered what God looks like? Have you ever wanted to see or at least hear God? Read 1 Kings 19:1-18.

What would you do if God told you that he was about to pass by? Would you be too scared to imagine what he may look or be like? Would you expect him to be in the powerful wind, an earthquake, or a fire?

The Bible says that the Lord was not in any of these things. Do you wonder how Elijah knew this? Why didn't he come out of the mouth of the cave to meet the majestic happenings within creation?

The gentle whisper spoke to Elijah. Elijah responded with humility, putting his cloak over his face, answering the Lord's questions.

Often, Christians want to see God. Perhaps this is because we feel that we need a life-altering event, a vision or experience that will drastically shape our faith. "Seeing is believing," some say—much of our understanding is influenced by what we see. But maybe we're looking too hard for the big events, the dramatic experiences, to hear the gentle whisper of God.

We can learn from God's gentleness. We, too, can present ourselves in a gentle way. God could have come to Elijah in any form, but he chose a gentle whisper.

Find a large seashell or a glass tumbler. Put your ear to the glass or shell. Can you hear the whisper? It sounds like the sea. Think about how you have to focus upon listening, upon hearing the whisper.

In many ways, this can remind us of how God speaks. Not with fire, loud crashing sounds, blasting trumpets, but with a subtle sound. As you continue to listen, thank God for his gentle presence. Pray that you will become gentle in demeanor, in word, in action, in presence.

HAVE YOU EVER WONDERE

What I saw, noticed, questioned, felt, read, thought, experienced:

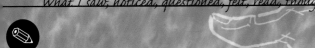

[write something]

Love. Joy. Peace. Patience. Kindness. Goodness. Faithfulness. **Gentleness.** Self-control.

{Whisper}

HAT GOD LOOKS LIKE?

Remote Control

Take a moment to find a remote control you use for your DVD player or VCR. Remove the batteries. Now try using it.

Even though you know *exactly* how to fix it, can you feel that tiny pinprick of discomfort as you aim the remote, click a button, and absolutely nothing happens?

That's because we *love* being in control. We want instant command of our time, our money, even our entertainment. We're big on being in charge.

But being able to control externals doesn't mean we can control ourselves. We're prone to flash judgments, harsh words, and poor decisions. We're constantly sabotaging our desire to lead Christlike lives.

Aim the remote control at your heart and push the "fast forward" arrow. Wouldn't it be great if that's all it took to instantly mature in your faith? Or if you could hit the "rewind" arrow whenever you wanted a second crack at correcting a mistake?

Place your useless remote aside and read Ephesians 4:1-32.

The fact is that growing in your ability to live out your faith takes time—*and* self-control. It's a choice to set aside your selfishness. To choose to be in relationship with others. To decide to live in ways that glorify God. To rely on the Holy Spirit to guide you. To do what God wants, no matter what.

Choosing. Deciding. Doing.

They're not automatic.

They take self-control.

(Note: If that remote control is something you share with the rest of your family, return the batteries after your devotional time!)

remote control

What I saw, noticed, questioned, felt, read, thought, experienced:

POWER

[write something]

TV/VIDEO

Love. Joy. Peace. Patience. Kindness. Goodness. Faithfulness. Gentleness. **Self-control.**

scorched Fingers

Fill up a glass of water and find a safe place to light a kitchen match—a wooden one is best. Hold the lit match so the flame burns steadily down the wooden shaft toward your fingers.

At *precisely* the moment the flame is about to singe your fingers, toss the match into the glass of water.

Act too quickly and you won't feel the warmth of the flame. Act too slowly and you'll learn why you aren't supposed to play with matches.

Self-control matters here. In life, it often does.

And the hardest place to control ourselves is often our thought life—*especially* when it comes to the opposite sex. We round the corner at school and our jaws drop. Our minds begin considering the possibilities.

What to do?

The Hebrew leader Joseph faced a similar situation when he was the victim of sexual harassment. His boss' wife suggested— actually *demanded*—that Joseph have sex with her. Day after day she persisted. Day after day he resisted. And when the situa-tion grew dangerous, Joseph turned and ran. Literally.

Read Genesis 39:1-20 now to see what happened.

Joseph's self-control kept him pure. Distanced him from temptation. Honored Go

But it *didn't* win him applause and admiratio His boss didn't believe Joseph, so Joseph was punished for a crime he didn't commit.

But Joseph's goal wasn't to please others c escape punishment. Joseph wanted to pleas God, no matter what—and his self-control helped Joseph overcome temptation.

How do you handle temptation? What sorts of temptations are so powerful that your self-control folds and you need to run? How would you have handled the encounter?

Your instincts told you when to extinguish the match—you sensed the danger. Like those instincts, the Holy Spirit enables you with the self-control you need to resist temptation when you need to, to flee when you need to.

What I saw, noticed, questioned, felt, read, thought, experienced:

[write something]

Love. Joy. Peace. Patience. Kindness. Goodness. Faithfulness. Gentleness. **Self-control.**

Bike Balance

How long has it been since you were on a bicycle? Even if you practically *live* on a bike, this activity may prove to be a challenge.

Find a bicycle and climb on. Roll it to a flat spot. Now place your feet on the pedals and sit up straight.

But don't move.

That's right—*don't* move. Not forward, backward, or sideways. Just balance—and sit.

Balancing on a bicycle takes tremendous self-control. Every twitch, every tensed muscle, shifts you ever so slightly—and can throw you to the ground.

Staying balanced, on a bike or in life, requires that you do two things that probably don't come naturally: slowing down and moving deliberately.

If you want to succeed in the Christian life, those are two attributes that will serve you well.

Slow down so you can hear God's voice. So you don't impulsively leap into situations or commitments without first knowing that's where God wants you to go.

Move deliberately, staying focused on what's most important.

Sounds simple, doesn't it? A balanced life in two simple steps.

Except it's not simple. Read Hebrews 12:1-13.

A Christlike life includes discipline. God disciplines you, and you discipline yourself.

The result?

Balance.

What I saw, noticed, questioned, felt, read, thought, experienced:

[write something]

?

Love. Joy. Peace. Patience. Kindness. Goodness. Faithfulness. Gentleness. **Self-control.**

Keep in Step

Have you ever participated in an old-fashioned three-legged race? Find a partner—a friend, neighbor, or family member—stand side by side, and tie one of your legs to one of his or hers. (Cloth works better than rope to tie; it's more comfortable.) Now try to walk, run, and maybe even skip.

Once you've finished, think about these questions. Was it difficult to keep in step? Did you fall down at first? Once you established a rhythm, was it easier to walk? Did it help to say words ("outside leg, inside leg") to keep you going?

Read Galatians 5:22-25. Read verse 25 aloud.

One important aspect about the fruit of the Spirit is that these are not gifts. Some people are not extra-blessed with patience, for example, leaving all the impatient people with extra joy. As Christians, filled with the Spirit, we can all have all of these fruits! But we must "keep in step with the Spirit."

What kind of relationship did you have with your three-legged-race partner? Often, people who have a stronger relationship can keep in step better in that game. Perhaps keeping in step with the Spirit is a lot like that. The better you know how to listen, how to communicate, the better you keep in step.

Fruit does take time to grow, though. Some years, trees need pruning, then after they're cut back, the fruit is more bountiful than ever. Don't get discouraged on the days you fail, because you will fail every day. But you will also succeed every day. This is a part of living by the Spirit. Read verse 25 a third time. Pray. Thank God for the fruit of his Spirit in your life.

What I saw, noticed, questioned, felt, read, thought, experienced:

[write something]

Love. Joy. Peace. Patience. Kindness. Goodness. Faithfulness. Gentleness. **Self-control.**

[goodbye]

Patience Kindness Goodness Faithfulness Gentleness Self-control Love Joy Peace Patience Kindness Gentleness Self-control Love Joy Peace Patience Kindness Goodness Faithfulness Love Joy Peace Patience Kindness Goodness Faithfulness Gentleness Self-control Love Joy Goodness Faithfulness Gentleness Self-control Love Joy Peace Patience Kindness Goodness Self-control Love Joy Peace Patience Kindness Goodness Faithfulness Gentleness Self-control Kindness Goodness Faithfulness Gentleness Self-control Love Joy Peace Patience Kindness Gentleness Self-control Love Joy Peace Patience Kindness Goodness Faithfulness Gentleness Patience Kindness Goodness Faithfulness Gentleness Self-control Love Joy Peace Patience Kindness Gentleness Self-control Love Joy Peace Patience Kindness Goodness Faithfulness Love Joy Peace Patience Kindness Goodness Faithfulness Gentleness Self-control Love Joy Goodness Faithfulness Gentleness Self-control Love Joy Peace Patience Kindness Goodness Self-control Love Joy Peace Patience Kindness Goodness Faithfulness Gentleness Self-control Kindness Goodness Faithfulness Gentleness Self-control Love Joy Peace Patience Kindness Kindness Self-control Love Joy Peace Patience Kindness Goodness Faithfulness Gentleness Patience Kindness Goodness Faithfulness Gentleness Self-control Love Joy Peace Patience Kindness Gentleness Self-control Love Joy Peace Patience Kindness Goodness Faithfulness Love Joy Peace Patience Kindness Goodness Faithfulness Gentleness Self-control Love Joy Goodness Faithfulness Gentleness Self-control Love Joy Peace Patience Kindness Goodness Self-control Love Joy Peace Patience Kindness Goodness Faithfulness Gentleness Self-control Kindness Goodness Faithfulness Gentleness Self-control Love Joy Peace Patience Kindness Kindness Self-control Love Joy Peace Patience Kindness Goodness Faithfulness Gentleness Patience Kindness Goodness Faithfulness Gentleness Self-control Love Joy Peace Patience Kindness Gentleness Self-control Love Joy Peace Patience Kindness Goodness Faithfulness Love Joy Peace Patience Kindness Goodness Faithfulness Gentleness Self-control Love Joy Goodness Faithfulness Gentleness Self-control Love Joy Peace Patience Kindness Goodness Self-control Love Joy Peace Patience Kindness Goodness Faithfulness Gentleness Self-control Kindness Goodness Faithfulness Gentleness Self-control Love Joy Peace Patience Kindness Goodness Self-control Love Joy Peace Patience Kindness Goodness Faithfulness Gentleness Patience Kindness Goodness Faithfulness Gentleness Self-control Love Joy Peace Patience Kindness Gentleness Self-control Love Joy Peace Patience Kindness Goodness Faithfulness Love Joy Peace Patience Kindness Goodness Faithfulness Gentleness Self-control Love Joy Goodness Faithfulness Gentleness Self-control Love Joy Peace Patience Kindness Goodness Self-control Love Joy Peace Patience Kindness Goodness Faithfulness Gentleness Self-control

Love. Joy. Peace. Patience. Kindness. Goodness. Faithfulness. Gentleness. Self-control. Love. Joy. Peace. Patience. Kindness. Goodness. Faithfulness. Gentleness. Self-control. Love. Joy. Peace. Patience. Kindness. Goodness. Faithfulness. Gentleness. Self-control. Love. Joy. Peace. Patience. Kindness. Goodness. Faithfulness. Gentleness. Self-control. Love. Joy. Peace. Patience. Kindness. Goodness. Faithfulness. Gentleness. Self-control. Love. Joy. Peace. Patience. Kindness. Goodness. Faithfulness. Gentleness. Self-control. Love. Joy. Peace. Patience. Kindness. Goodness. Faithfulness. Gentleness. Self-control. Love. Joy. Peace. Patience. Kindness. Goodness. Faithfulness. Gentleness. Self-control. Love. Joy. Peace. Patience. Kindness. Goodness. Faithfulness. Gentleness. Self-control. Love. Joy. Peace. Patience. Kindness. Goodness. Faithfulness. Gentleness. Self-control. Love. Joy. Peace. Patience. Kindness. Goodness. Faithfulness. Gentleness. Self-control. Love. Joy. Peace. Patience. Kindness. Goodness. Faithfulness. Gentleness. Self-control. Love. Joy. Peace. Patience. Kindness. Goodness. Faithfulness. Gentleness. Self-control. Love. Joy. Peace. Patience. Kindness. Goodness. Faithfulness. Gentleness. Self-control. Love. Joy. Peace. Patience. Kindness. Goodness. Faithfulness. Gentleness. Self-control. Love. Joy. Peace. Patience. Kindness. Goodness. Faithfulness. Gentleness. Self-control. Love. Joy. Peace. Patience. Kindness. Goodness. Faithfulness. Gentleness. Self-control. Love. Joy. Peace. Patience. Kindness. Goodness. Faithfulness. Gentleness. Self-control. Love. Joy. Peace. Patience. Kindness. Goodness. Faithfulness. Gentleness. Self-control. Love. Joy. Peace. Patience. Kindness. Goodness. Faithfulness. Gentleness. Self-control. Love. Joy. Peace. Patience. Kindness. Goodness. Faithfulness. Gentleness. Self-control. Love. Joy. Peace. Patience. Kindness. Goodness. Faithfulness. Gentleness. Self-control. Love. Joy. Peace. Patience. Kindness. Goodness. Faithfulness. Gentleness. Self-control. Love. Joy. Peace. Patience. Kindness. Goodness. Faithfulness. Gentleness. Self-control. Love. Joy. Peace. Patience. Kindness. Goodness. Faithfulness. Gentleness. Self-control. Love. Joy. Peace. Patience. Kindness. Goodness. Faithfulness. Gentleness. Self-control. Love. Joy. Peace. Patience. Kindness. Goodness. Faithfulness. Gentleness. Self-control. Love. Joy. Peace. Patience. Kindness. Goodness. Faithfulness. Gentleness. Self-control. Love. Joy. Peace. Patience. Kindness. Goodness. Faithfulness. Gentleness. Self-control. Love. Joy. Peace. Patience. Kindness. Goodness. Faithfulness. Gentleness. Self-control. Love. Joy. Peace. Patience. Kindness. Goodness. Faithfulness. Gentleness. Self-control. Love. Joy. Peace. Patience. Kindness. Goodness. Faithfulness. Gentleness. Self-control. Love. Joy. Peace. Patience. Kindness. Goodness. Faithfulness. Gentleness. Self-control. Love. Joy.